NATIONAL
GEOGRAPHIC
School Publishing

Our Place in Space

Bilal Jouhar

PICTURE CREDITS
Cover, 4 (all), 5 (above left), 7 (all), 9 (right), 14, 17 (below), 18 (left), 19 (all), 21 (left), NASA; 1, 2, 5 (right), 8, 10, 11, 12 (right), 13 (all), 15, 16, 17 (above and inset above), 18 (right), 20 (left), 21 (right), Photolibrary.com; 6–7, Guy Holt Illustration; 9 (left), 12 (left), Getty Images; 17 (right), APL/Corbis; 20 (right), AGStockUSA,Inc./Alamy.

Produced through the worldwide resources of the National Geographic Society, John M. Fahey, Jr., President and Chief Executive Officer; Gilbert M. Grosvenor, Chairman of the Board; Nina D. Hoffman, Executive Vice President and President, Books and Education Publishing Group.

PREPARED BY NATIONAL GEOGRAPHIC SCHOOL PUBLISHING
Steve Mico, Executive Vice President and Publisher, Children's Books and Education Publishing Group; Marianne Hiland, Editor in Chief; Lynnette Brent, Executive Editor; Michael Murphy and Barbara Wood, Senior Editors; Nicole Rouse, Editor; Bea Jackson, Design Director; David Dumo, Art Director; Shanin Glenn, Designer; Margaret Sidlosky, Illustrations Director; Matt Wascavage, Manager of Publishing Services; Sean Philpotts, Production Manager.

MANUFACTURING AND QUALITY MANAGEMENT
Christopher A. Liedel, Chief Financial Officer; Phillip L. Schlosser, Vice President; Clifton M. Brown III, Director.

BOOK DEVELOPMENT
Ibis for Kids Australia Pty Limited.

Published by the National Geographic Society
1145 17th Street, N.W.
Washington, D.C. 20036-4688

Product No. 4W1005068

ISBN-13: 978-1-4263-5064-1
ISBN-10: 1-4263-5064-3

2010 2009
3 4 5 6 7 8 9 10 11 12 13 14 15

Printed in China

Contents

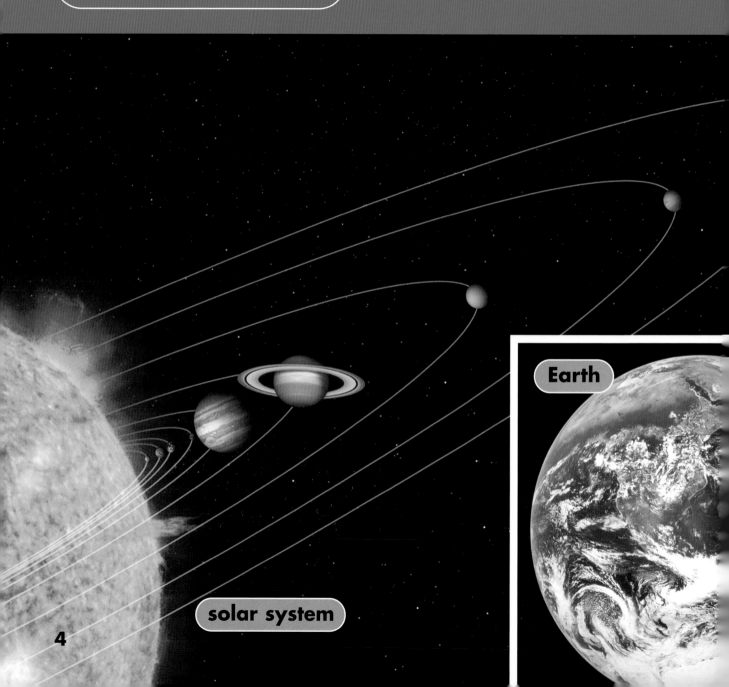

Earth

solar system

4

What do you know about Earth and our solar system? What else do you know about space?

astronaut

stars

moon

Our Planet

We live on Earth. Earth is a **planet** that **orbits** the sun. The sun gives Earth light and warmth.

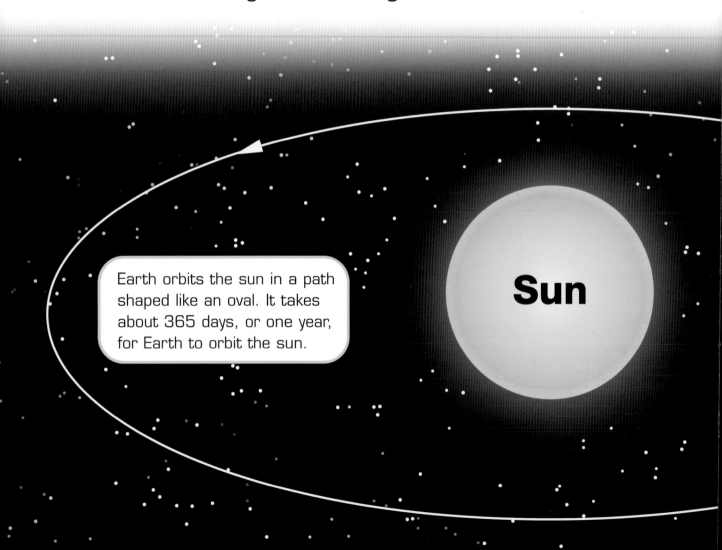

Earth orbits the sun in a path shaped like an oval. It takes about 365 days, or one year, for Earth to orbit the sun.

Sun

As Earth orbits the sun, it also **rotates**, or spins. As Earth rotates, different parts of its surface face the sun. On the part of Earth that faces the sun, it is day.

Earth

Earth's Moon

Our moon orbits Earth. It takes about 27 days for the moon to travel all the way around Earth.

The moon does not produce any light of its own. The moon appears to shine because it reflects light from the sun. We only see the part of the moon that is lit by the sun.

The **atmosphere** is the air that surrounds Earth. It keeps Earth from getting too hot or too cold. Air, water, warmth, and light make life possible on Earth.

Earth's atmosphere provides air for people and animals to breathe.

Much of Earth is covered with water. People, animals, and plants need water to survive.

Gravity

Gravity is a force that pulls things toward Earth. It keeps us on the ground. Without gravity, objects on Earth would float.

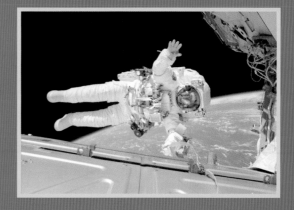

In space, the force of gravity is weaker than it is on Earth. This is why astronauts float in space.

Our Solar System

Earth is just one planet in our **solar system**. There are eight other planets that orbit the sun. The other planets are very different from Earth.

The sun is the center of our solar system. It is a star. Like all stars, it is made of burning **gases**.

- Pluto
- Neptune
- Uranus
- Saturn
- Jupiter
- Mars
- Earth
- Venus
- Mercury

Mercury is the closest planet to the sun. Pluto is the farthest away.

The Biggest Planet

Jupiter is the biggest planet in our solar system. It is about as wide as 11 Earths. Jupiter is made of gases. It is one of four planets known as the gas giants. The other gas giants are Saturn, Uranus, and Neptune.

There are objects in our solar system besides the sun and planets. There are also asteroids, comets, and meteors.

Asteroids are pieces of rock that orbit the sun.

A comet is a ball of dirt and ice with a tail of gas and dust.

A meteor is a piece of metal or rock that travels into Earth's atmosphere. It becomes so hot that it glows.

A meteor that reaches Earth's surface is called a meteorite. This crater was made when a meteorite crashed into Earth thousands of years ago.

Our Galaxy

Our solar system is part of the Milky Way **galaxy**. There are billions of stars in our galaxy. There are also huge clouds of gas and dust.

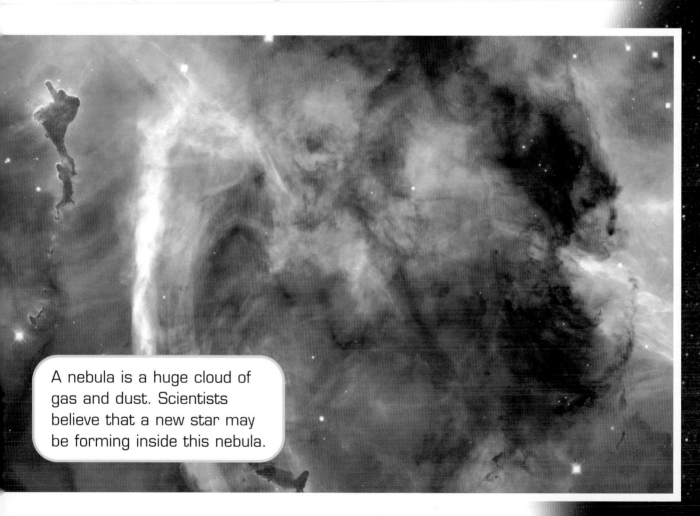

A nebula is a huge cloud of gas and dust. Scientists believe that a new star may be forming inside this nebula.

Most of the stars we see at night are part of our galaxy. Some stars are so far away that we can't see them.

Exploring Space

Scientists use telescopes to find out about our solar system and our galaxy. There is even a telescope that orbits Earth!

A telescope makes far-away things look bigger. People use telescopes to study space.

The Hubble space telescope orbits Earth. It takes pictures of things in space and sends them to Earth.

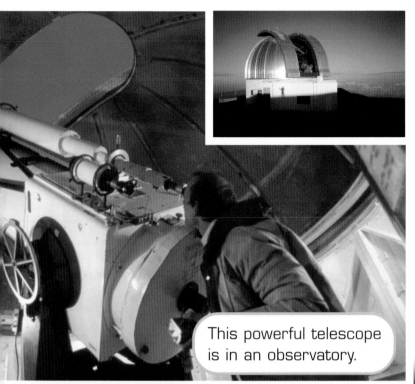

This powerful telescope is in an observatory.

Galileo

About 400 years ago, Galileo Galilei was the first person to use a telescope to look into space. He used it to learn about the moon. Galileo was the first person to see that the surface of the moon has craters and mountains.

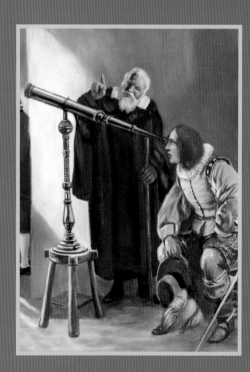

Scientists also use **spacecraft** to learn about space. Sometimes astronauts travel on the spacecraft.

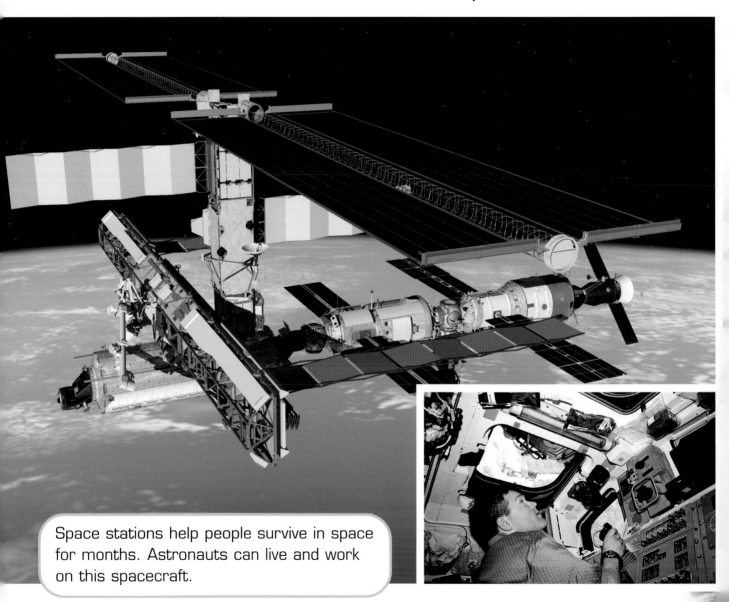

Space stations help people survive in space for months. Astronauts can live and work on this spacecraft.

Sometimes astronauts leave the spacecraft. Outside the spacecraft, astronauts need special clothes and breathing equipment to survive.

This drawing shows a spacecraft that was built to explore the surface of Mars.

Talk about these pictures.
What do you know about our place in space?

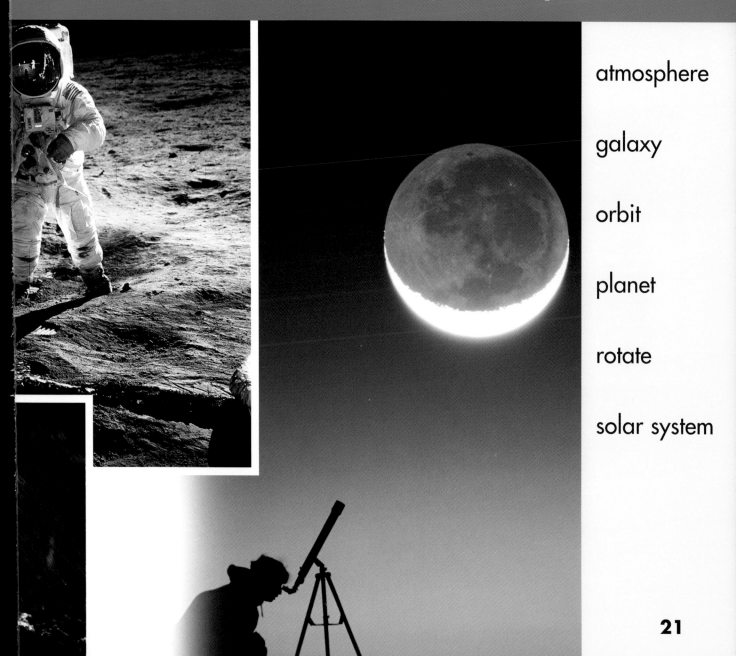

atmosphere

galaxy

orbit

planet

rotate

solar system

Glossary

atmosphere (page 8)
The air that surrounds Earth
Earth's atmosphere provides air for people to breathe.

galaxy (page 14)
A large group of stars
From Earth, we can see many of the stars in our galaxy.

gas (page 10)
A substance that does not have a definite shape or size
The air we breathe is made up of gases.

orbit (page 6)
To travel around a planet or star
Mercury is a planet that orbits the sun.

planet (page 6)
An object that orbits the sun or another star
Jupiter is one of the planets in our solar system.

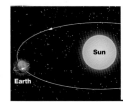

rotate (page 7)
To spin around
We have day and night because Earth rotates.

solar system (page 10)
A group of planets and other objects that orbit a star
Saturn is a planet in our solar system.

spacecraft (page 18)
A vehicle that is sent into space
Scientists can use spacecraft to learn about other planets.

Index